DAILY HABITS FOR A HAPPIER YOU

HAPPIER YOU

SMALL CHANGES FOR BIG IMPACT

BY MANDY ADAMS

CONTENTS

Introduction – Setting the Foundation for Happiness ...5

Chapter 2. The Science of Happiness-Unveiling the Secret of Joy ...11

Chapter 3. Morning Rituals for a Positive Start- Waking Up to Happiness ...18

Chapter 4. Mindful Living Throughout the Day- Cultivating Awareness in Every Moment ...27

Chapter 5. The Power of Gratitude- Transforming Your Life Through Gratefulness ...37

Chapter 6. Nurturing Relationships- The Art of Cultivating Connection ...46

Chapter 7. Finding Joy in Work and Passion- Crafting a Fulfilling Career and Pursuing What Sets Your Soul on Fire 57

Chapter 8. Physical Well-Being for a Happy Mind- Nourishing Your Body, Energizing Your Spirit ...68

Chapter 9. Embracing Imperfection- The Art of Celebrating Your Beautiful Flaws ...78

Chapter 10. Sustaining Happiness for a Lifetime- A Joyful Journey Into Forever Smiles ...88

Introduction – Setting the Foundation for Happiness

Hey there, fellow happiness seeker! Welcome to the very beginning of our journey toward a brighter, more joyful life. In this opening chapter, we're going to lay down the groundwork for the adventure ahead, exploring the incredible world of daily habits and their profound impact on our overall happiness.

Discovering the Happiness Quest

Let's start by asking a simple yet profound question: What does happiness mean to you? It's a term tossed around a lot, but its definition can be as unique as the individual pondering it. Happiness might be found in the warmth of connections with loved ones, the pursuit of personal goals, or the simple pleasures of everyday life.

Our journey together revolves around the idea that happiness isn't a distant destination but a path we walk every day. It's not about grand gestures or momentous events; instead, it's about the small, consistent actions that shape our lives. This book is your guide to making those little tweaks, those daily adjustments that can create a substantial impact on your overall well-being.

The Power of Habits

Now, let's talk about habits. We all have them, from the way we brush our teeth in the morning to how we unwind before bedtime. They're the autopilot settings that govern our daily lives. But what if we could tweak these habits just a bit to make them work in our favor? That's where the magic happens.

Understanding the science behind habits is like getting the keys to your own happiness kingdom. We'll delve into the fascinating world of habit formation, exploring how our brains work and how we can leverage this knowledge to cultivate habits that lead to a happier, more fulfilled life.

A Blueprint for Change

This book isn't about reinventing yourself overnight. It's about acknowledging the power of small changes. Think of it as a blueprint for building a happier version of yourself, one habit at a time. We'll explore habits that are not only easy to adopt but also sustainable in the long run. After all, the key to lasting happiness lies in consistency.

Why Should You Care?

You might be wondering, "Why should I bother making changes to my routine? Is happiness really that big a deal?" Well, buckle up, because the answer is a resounding yes! The pursuit of happiness isn't a frivolous endeavor; it's a fundamental aspect of the human experience.

We'll take a peek into the science of happiness, exploring how neurotransmitters like serotonin and dopamine play a role in our mood and well-being. Understanding the science behind happiness isn't just fascinating; it's the key to unlocking a life filled with more joy and satisfaction.

What to Expect

In the chapters ahead, we'll journey through various aspects of your daily life, uncovering habits that can turn your ordinary days into extraordinary ones. From morning rituals that set a positive tone for the day to the magic of mindful living and the transformative power of gratitude, we've got it all covered.

Relationships, work, physical well-being, and the liberating embrace of imperfection—all these pieces come together to form the mosaic of a happier life. We'll explore each one, offering practical tips, real-life examples, and a friendly nudge to inspire positive change.

Your Adventure Begins Now

So, are you ready to embark on this adventure? Are you ready to explore the untapped potential within your daily habits and unleash the power of happiness? If your answer is a resounding "yes," then you're in the right place.

This book is your companion, your cheerleader, and your guide. It's not about perfection; it's about progress. It's about discovering what works for you, celebrating the small victories, and embracing the journey toward a happier you.

As we dive into the chapters that follow, remember that change is a gradual process. Be kind to yourself, celebrate the wins, and keep moving forward. Your happiness is worth the effort, and this book is here to support you every step of the way.

So, dear reader, let's turn the page and begin this exciting journey together. Here's to daily habits, small changes, and the boundless joy that awaits us on the path to a happier you!

CHAPTER 2. THE SCIENCE OF HAPPINESS-UNVEILING THE SECRET OF JOY

Hey there, happiness explorer! Welcome to the intriguing world of Chapter 2, where we're going to unravel the mysteries behind happiness. Get ready to dive deep into the science of what makes us smile, laugh, and feel that warm, fuzzy glow inside.

The Happiness Puzzle

Imagine happiness as a complex puzzle, and science is the key to understanding how the pieces fit together. In this chapter, we'll explore the fascinating research that delves into the inner workings of our brains, the chemistry behind our emotions, and the profound impact it all has on our daily lives.

Neurotransmitters and the Feel-Good Factor

Let's start our journey with the brain's best friends: neurotransmitters. These tiny messengers play a crucial role in regulating our mood and emotions. One of the VIPs in this feel-good parade is serotonin, often referred to as the "happiness neurotransmitter." It's like the conductor of the orchestra, orchestrating the symphony of emotions that make us feel content and satisfied.

Dopamine, another rockstar neurotransmitter, takes center stage when it comes to pleasure and reward. Ever experienced that burst of joy after achieving a goal or enjoying a delicious meal? Thank dopamine for that delightful sensation.

Understanding these neurotransmitters isn't just about academic curiosity; it's the key to unlocking ways to boost our mood naturally. From simple lifestyle changes to cultivating habits that promote the production of these happy chemicals, we've got the insider scoop on how to keep the good vibes flowing.

Positive Psychology and the Pursuit of Well-Being

Enter positive psychology, the science that flips the script on traditional psychology's focus on pathology and dysfunction. Positive psychology shines a spotlight on what makes life worth living, emphasizing strengths, virtues, and factors that contribute to a fulfilling existence.

We'll explore the principles of positive psychology that provide a roadmap for our journey toward happiness. From cultivating gratitude to savoring positive experiences, these principles are like signposts guiding us toward a brighter, more joyful life.

The Impact of Thoughts on Emotions

Ever heard the saying, "Change your thoughts, and you change your world"? Well, there's a nugget of wisdom in those words. Our thoughts have a powerful influence on our emotions, shaping our perception of the world around us. In this chapter, we'll uncover the connection between thoughts and emotions, and how tweaking our mindset can lead to a more positive and fulfilling life.

The Happiness Set Point

Now, let's talk about the happiness set point—a sort of baseline for our well-being. Research suggests that regardless of life circumstances, we each have a natural predisposition for happiness. The good news? This set point isn't fixed. Through intentional practices and habit formation, we can nudge that set point upward, steering our lives toward greater joy.

Practical Strategies for a Happier Brain

Alright, let's get practical. What can you do, starting today, to boost your happiness levels? We've got a treasure trove of actionable strategies, from simple daily habits to mindset shifts that can make a world of difference.

1. *Gratitude Practices:* The simple act of counting your blessings can have a profound impact on your mood. Whether it's keeping a gratitude journal or expressing thanks to those around you, gratitude is like a magnet for joy.

2. *Acts of Kindness:* The joy of giving is a real thing. Engaging in acts of kindness, big or small, not only benefits others but also provides a significant happiness boost. It's a win-win!

3. *Savoring Positive Experiences:* Ever rushed through a beautiful sunset without really

savoring the moment? We've all been there. Learn the art of slowing down, appreciating the good times, and letting those positive experiences linger.

4. *Mindfulness and Meditation:* In the hustle and bustle of modern life, our minds can feel like a crowded subway during rush hour. Mindfulness and meditation offer a ticket to a calmer, more centered state of being.

Happiness in Action: Real-Life Stories

To bring these concepts to life, we'll dive into the stories of real people who have transformed their lives through the science of happiness. From individuals who overcame adversity to those who discovered joy in the midst of everyday routines, these stories serve as beacons of inspiration on our collective journey toward a happier existence.

The Quest Continues

As we wrap up this chapter, keep in mind that the pursuit of happiness is not a one-size-fits-all journey.

What works for one person may not work for another. That's the beauty of our individuality.

So, fellow happiness enthusiast, let's take this newfound knowledge and apply it to our lives. Experiment with different strategies, embrace the ebb and flow of emotions, and remember that the pursuit of happiness is a lifelong quest—one that's worth every twist, turn, and discovery along the way.

In the next chapters, we'll delve into specific habits and practices that align with the science of happiness. Get ready to turn that knowledge into action, because the best chapters of our happiness story are yet to be written. Until then, keep smiling, keep exploring, and keep embracing the joy that surrounds you!

CHAPTER 3. MORNING RITUALS FOR A POSITIVE START- WAKING UP TO HAPPINESS

Good morning, sunshine! Welcome to a chapter that's all about kickstarting your day with a burst of positivity. We're diving into the magical realm of morning rituals—those intentional habits that can set the tone for a day filled with joy, purpose, and all-around good vibes.

The Power of Mornings

Ever heard the phrase, "How you start your day is how you live your day"? Well, it turns out there's a lot of truth to that. Mornings lay the foundation for the hours that follow, and incorporating positive habits during this time can create a ripple effect that lasts throughout the day.

Rise and Shine: Crafting Your Ideal Morning Routine

Let's start by crafting a morning routine that's tailor-made for you. It's not about cramming in a laundry list of activities but about curating a sequence that aligns with your preferences and energizes you for the day ahead.

1. *Wake Up with Intent:* Say goodbye to the snooze button and hello to waking up with purpose. Set a positive intention for the day as soon as you open your eyes. It could be as simple as expressing gratitude for a new day or setting a personal goal to focus on.

2. *Hydration Ritual:* Before diving into the chaos of the day, treat your body to a refreshing glass of water. It's like giving your internal system a gentle wake-up call and sets the stage for proper hydration throughout the day.

3. *Move Your Body:* Whether it's a full-blown workout, a few stretches, or a dance party in your living room, get your body moving. Physical activity not only boosts energy levels but also releases those feel-good endorphins.

4. *Mindfulness Moments:* Incorporate mindfulness into your morning, even if it's just for a few minutes. It could be through meditation, deep breathing exercises, or simply savoring your morning cup of tea or coffee in peaceful contemplation.

5. *Nourish Your Body:* Breakfast is the fuel that powers your day. Choose foods that provide sustained energy, and take a moment to savor each bite. It's not just about physical nourishment but also about savoring the sensory experience.

6. *Set Priorities:* Take a few minutes to glance at your schedule and set priorities for the day. This helps create a sense of direction and prevents the feeling of being overwhelmed by tasks later on.

Mindful Mornings: A Deep Dive

Now, let's take a closer look at a couple of these morning rituals and understand why they hold the key to a positive start.

1. Wake Up with Intent:

Imagine starting your day with a clear sense of purpose. It's like putting on a pair of glasses that filter out the unnecessary noise and bring your focus to what truly matters. Whether you express gratitude, set daily affirmations, or visualize your goals, waking up with intent is like turning on the guiding beacon for your day.

2. Hydration Ritual:

Our bodies are like well-oiled machines that need hydration to function optimally. After a night of rest, your body is in a slight state of dehydration, and a glass of water in the morning kickstarts your internal engines. Plus, there's something refreshing about that first sip—it's like a morning hug for your insides.

3. Move Your Body:

Exercise doesn't have to mean an hour at the gym (unless that's your jam). It could be a short yoga session, a brisk walk, or a quick set of jumping jacks. The goal is to get your blood flowing and wake up your muscles. The bonus? The release of endorphins, those natural mood lifters that set a positive tone for the day.

4. Mindfulness Moments:

In the hustle and bustle of life, finding moments of stillness is a gift to yourself. Whether you practice meditation, deep breathing, or simply take a moment to appreciate the quietude, mindfulness anchors you in the present. It's a pause button for the mind, allowing you to approach the day with clarity and calm.

Real-Life Morning Transformations

To inspire you on your morning ritual journey, let's delve into the stories of individuals who witnessed remarkable transformations by embracing intentional morning habits.

Sarah's Gratitude Journal: Sarah, a busy professional juggling work and family responsibilities, felt overwhelmed and stressed. She decided to start a gratitude journal as part of her morning routine. Each day, she wrote down three things she was grateful for. Over time, this simple practice shifted her focus from what was lacking to the abundance in her life. The result? A more positive outlook and increased resilience in the face of challenges.

Mike's Sunrise Walks: Mike, an entrepreneur with a hectic schedule, felt the need for a morning ritual that connected him with nature. He started waking up early for sunrise walks in a nearby park. This not only provided him with a dose of fresh air and exercise but also became a meditative time for reflection. The sunrise symbolized a new beginning, and Mike found that these morning walks set a positive tone for his entire day.

Overcoming Morning Hurdles

Now, let's address the elephant in the room—the challenges that often accompany the quest for a positive morning routine.

Time Constraints:

In a world that seems to be in perpetual fast-forward, finding time for morning rituals can be challenging. The key is to start small. Even dedicating 10-15 minutes to intentional activities can make a significant difference. Remember, it's about quality, not quantity.

Resisting Change:

Our comfort zones are cozy, but growth happens when we step out of them. If the idea of changing your morning routine feels daunting, start with one small change at a time. Gradual adjustments are more sustainable and allow you to ease into a new rhythm.

Flexibility is Key:

Life is unpredictable, and not every morning will go according to plan. Be flexible and forgiving. If your usual routine gets disrupted, find ways to adapt. The goal is to cultivate a positive start, not to add stress to your day.

Your Personal Morning Symphony

As we wrap up this chapter, picture your morning routine as a symphony—a harmonious blend of intentional actions that create a masterpiece. Whether you're a fan of classical compositions or prefer the upbeat tempo of pop, your morning routine is uniquely yours.

Experiment with different elements, discover what resonates with you, and feel free to improvise. This chapter is an invitation to compose your morning symphony, a melody that resonates with joy, purpose, and positive energy.

So, dear reader, tomorrow morning, as you greet the sun and embark on a new day, remember that the first notes of your day can set the rhythm for the entire composition. Embrace the power of morning rituals, and let the music of positivity fill your day. Until then, rise and shine, and may your mornings be as delightful as the possibilities that await you!

Chapter 4. Mindful Living Throughout the Day- Cultivating Awareness in Every Moment

Hello, mindful adventurer! Welcome to a chapter that's all about infusing your day with a dash of mindfulness. In the hustle and bustle of our lives, it's easy to get caught up in the chaos. But fear not—we're about to explore the art of mindful living, a practice that can transform your ordinary day into an extraordinary journey of presence and joy.

The Mindfulness Magic

So, what exactly is mindfulness? It's not about escaping to a mountaintop to meditate for hours (though, if that's your thing, go for it!). Mindfulness is the art of being present in the moment, fully engaged in what you're doing without judgment. It's about savoring the richness of each experience, no matter how mundane it may seem.

The Power of Now

Mindfulness invites us to embrace the power of now. Often, our minds are time travelers, jumping between the regrets of yesterday and the anxieties of tomorrow. But the present moment—the now—is where life unfolds. In this chapter, we'll explore how to anchor ourselves in the present, bringing a sense of peace and clarity to our daily lives.

Mindful Living: Beyond Meditation

While meditation is a powerful tool for cultivating mindfulness, the practice extends far beyond the cushion. Mindful living is about infusing awareness into every aspect of your day, from the mundane to the meaningful. Let's embark on a journey through the day, exploring how mindfulness can be woven into the fabric of your existence.

Mindful Mornings: A Continuation

Our morning routine, as we explored in the previous chapter, sets the stage for the day. Now, let's dive deeper into how mindfulness can be integrated into these early hours.

1. _Mindful Hydration:_ Remember that glass of water you enjoyed in the morning? Take a moment to savor it. Feel the coolness as it touches your lips, appreciate the refreshing taste, and be present in this simple act of nourishing your body.

2. _Mindful Movement:_ Whether you're stretching, doing yoga, or going for a morning walk, bring mindfulness to your movements. Feel the stretch in your muscles, the rhythm of your breath, and the sensation of each step. It's not just physical activity; it's a dance with the present moment.

3. _Mindful Breakfast:_ As you eat your breakfast, resist the urge to multitask. Instead, savor each bite. Notice the flavors, textures, and the nourishment your meal provides. It's a mindful feast for your senses.

Mindfulness at Work: Navigating the Day

For many of us, a significant portion of the day is spent at work. Whether you're in an office, working remotely, or pursuing creative endeavors, mindfulness can be a game-changer in the professional realm.

1. _Mindful Transitions:_ Before diving into a new task or project, take a moment to transition mindfully. Close your eyes, take a deep breath, and consciously let go of the previous activity. It's like hitting the reset button for your focus.

2. _Single-Tasking:_ In a world that glorifies multitasking, mindfulness champions the art of single-tasking. Focus your attention on one task at a time, bringing your full presence to the activity. You'll be amazed at the depth of your engagement and the quality of your work.

3. _Mindful Breaks:_ Breaks are not just for scrolling through social media or checking emails. Use your breaks as opportunities for mini-mindfulness sessions. Step outside, take a few mindful breaths, or simply enjoy a moment of stillness.

Mindfulness in Communication: Building Joyful Connections

Communication forms the heartbeat of our relationships, and mindfulness can enrich the way we connect with others.

1. _Deep Listening:_ Instead of formulating your response while someone is speaking, practice deep listening. Give your full attention to the speaker, and let their words land before crafting your reply. It's a gift of presence.

2. _Mindful Speech:_ Before speaking, take a moment to consider your words. Are they kind, necessary, and true? Mindful speech is about communicating with intention and compassion.

3. _Pause and Respond:_ In moments of tension or disagreement, resist the urge to react impulsively. Take a mindful pause, breathe, and respond thoughtfully. It's a powerful way to navigate challenging conversations.

Mindfulness in Everyday Activities: Finding Joy in the Ordinary

Our day is filled with a multitude of activities, from doing household chores to running errands. These seemingly mundane moments are ripe for mindfulness.

1. *Mindful Walking:* Whether you're walking to the mailbox or strolling through the grocery store, bring awareness to each step. Feel the ground beneath you, notice the movement of your body, and relish the act of walking.

2. *Mindful Chores:* Turning mundane chores into mindfulness practices can be surprisingly enjoyable. Whether you're washing dishes, folding laundry, or sweeping the floor, approach the task with full attention. It's a form of moving meditation.

3. *Gratitude in Action:* Infuse everyday activities with gratitude. As you engage in routine tasks, express gratitude for the functionality of your body, the shelter of your home, and the abundance of your life. It's a transformative perspective shift.

Overcoming Mindfulness Hurdles

While the benefits of mindfulness are vast, incorporating it into your daily life may come with its challenges. Let's address some common hurdles and explore how to navigate them.

Mind-Wandering Mind: Our minds have a tendency to wander, and that's perfectly normal. When you notice your thoughts drifting, gently guide them back to the present moment. It's a practice of patience and self-compassion.

Time Constraints: Feeling like you don't have time for mindfulness is a common obstacle. Remember, mindfulness doesn't require hours of practice. Even a few minutes scattered throughout the day can make a significant impact.

Resistance to Silence: In a world buzzing with noise, silence can be intimidating. Start with short moments of silence and gradually extend the duration as you become more comfortable. Silence is where mindfulness often speaks the loudest.

Mindful Reflection: A Daily Practice

As the day winds down, take a few moments for mindful reflection. It's a simple yet profound practice that allows you to review your day with kindness and curiosity.

1. _Reflect on Gratitude:_ Take note of moments that brought you joy, gratitude, or a sense of accomplishment. It could be a small gesture, a connection with a loved one, or a personal achievement.

2. _Acknowledge Challenges:_ Instead of dwelling on difficulties, acknowledge them with a compassionate mindset. What did you learn from challenges, and how can they contribute to your growth?

3. _Set Intentions for Tomorrow:_ As you wrap up the day, set positive intentions for tomorrow. What mindful habits do you want to carry forward, and how can you enhance your presence in the upcoming day?

Your Mindful Journey Continues

As we conclude this chapter, remember that mindfulness is a journey, not a destination. It's about savoring the richness of each moment, embracing the ebb and flow of life, and finding joy in the ordinary.

So, dear reader, as you continue your mindful journey, may each step be a dance with the present moment, and may each breath be a reminder of the beauty that surrounds you. In the next chapters, we'll explore more ways to infuse your life with mindfulness, creating a tapestry of presence and joy. Until then, breathe, be present, and let the magic of mindfulness unfold in your day.

Chapter 5. The Power of Gratitude- Transforming Your Life Through Gratefulness

Get ready to dive into a chapter that's all about unlocking the transformative magic of gratitude. It's not just a fleeting emotion; it's a powerhouse that has the potential to reshape your outlook on life, relationships, and your overall sense of well-being.

The Gratitude Revolution

Gratitude is more than just saying "thank you" when someone holds the door for you or hands you a cup of coffee. It's a revolutionary way of experiencing the world, a lens through which you can view your life with fresh eyes. In this chapter, we'll embark on a journey through the landscapes of gratitude, exploring how this simple yet profound practice can become a cornerstone of your daily life.

Gratitude 101: What It Is and Why It Matters

So, what exactly is gratitude? At its core, gratitude is the practice of recognizing and appreciating the positive aspects of life, both big and small. It's about shifting our focus from what we lack to what we have, from complaints to celebrations.

Why does it matter, you ask? Well, the benefits of gratitude are like a treasure trove waiting to be discovered:

1. *Improved Mental Health:* Gratitude has been linked to reduced stress, anxiety, and depression. It acts as a natural mood enhancer, creating a positive ripple effect on your mental well-being.

2. *Enhanced Relationships:* Expressing gratitude fosters a deeper connection with others. It strengthens relationships, builds trust, and contributes to an atmosphere of positivity.

3. *Physical Health Boost:* Believe it or not, practicing gratitude can have tangible effects on your physical health. It's associated with better sleep, lower blood pressure, and a strengthened immune system.

4. *Increased Resilience:* Grateful individuals tend to navigate challenges with greater resilience. When faced with adversity, they are more likely to find silver linings and opportunities for growth.

The Gratitude Habit: From Thankfulness to Transformation

Now that we understand the what and why of gratitude, let's explore how to turn it from a sporadic emotion into a daily habit—one that can transform your life.

1. *Gratitude Journaling:* The classic and incredibly effective gratitude practice. Each day, take a few moments to jot down things you're grateful for. They can be as simple as a warm cup of tea, a kind word from a friend, or the sunshine peeking through the clouds.

2. *Gratitude Rituals:* Create simple rituals around gratitude. It could be expressing thanks before a meal, reflecting on the day's blessings before bedtime, or incorporating gratitude into your

morning routine. Rituals anchor gratitude in your daily life.

3. *Expressing Gratitude to Others:* Don't keep your gratitude to yourself. Express it to the people who make a positive impact on your life. Whether it's a heartfelt thank-you note, a phone call, or a face-to-face expression of appreciation, sharing gratitude amplifies its effects.

Gratitude in Action: Real-Life Stories

Let's delve into the stories of individuals whose lives were transformed by the power of gratitude.

Emily's Gratitude Jar: Feeling overwhelmed by the demands of her job and personal life, Emily decided to create a gratitude jar. Each day, she would write down one thing she was grateful for on a small piece of paper and put it in the jar. Over time, the jar filled up with moments of joy, love, and simple pleasures. On challenging days, Emily would revisit her gratitude jar, and it became a tangible reminder of the abundance in her life.

James's Gratitude Walks: James, a nature enthusiast, incorporated gratitude into his daily walks. As he strolled through parks and green spaces, he would express gratitude for the beauty of nature, the fresh air, and the ability to move his body. These gratitude walks not only became a source of joy but also deepened his connection with the natural world.

Gratitude and Relationships

The impact of gratitude extends beyond personal well-being—it weaves its magic into the fabric of our relationships.

1. *Cultivating a Culture of Appreciation:* In any relationship, be it romantic, familial, or friendships, expressing gratitude creates a culture of appreciation. It's a way of saying, "I see you, and I value you."

2. *Navigating Challenges with Gratitude:* When conflicts arise, approaching them with a mindset of gratitude can be transformative. Instead of focusing on grievances, look for aspects of the

relationship that bring joy and connection. It's a powerful tool for conflict resolution.

3. _Gratitude in Romantic Relationships:_ In romantic relationships, expressing gratitude for your partner's qualities, gestures, and presence strengthens the bond. It's the glue that holds the relationship together during both sunny and stormy days.

Overcoming Gratitude Challenges

While the benefits of gratitude are clear, incorporating it into our lives may not always be smooth sailing. Let's address common challenges and explore strategies for overcoming them.

The "Not Enough Time" Challenge: In a fast-paced world, finding time for gratitude practices might seem like a luxury. The key is to start small. Dedicate just a few minutes each day to gratitude journaling or expressing thanks. Remember, consistency is more important than duration.

Gratitude Amidst Challenges: During tough times, practicing gratitude may feel counterintuitive. However, it's precisely during challenges that gratitude can be a powerful ally. Instead of denying difficulties, acknowledge them, and also look for aspects of your life that bring comfort and support.

Overcoming Habitual Negativity: If negativity has become a habit, shifting towards gratitude might initially feel like a stretch. Start by noticing small positive moments and gradually expand your awareness. It's a process of rewiring your mindset over time.

Gratitude as a Lifestyle

As we wrap up this chapter, consider gratitude not as a fleeting emotion but as a lifestyle—a way of approaching each day with a heart full of appreciation. Whether you're expressing thanks for the warmth of sunlight, the laughter of loved ones, or the lessons learned from challenges, gratitude is a transformative force.

So, dear reader, let gratitude become your daily companion. Let it infuse your life with positivity, deepen your connections, and be a guiding light during both ordinary and extraordinary moments. As we continue our journey, let's carry the magic of gratitude with us, turning each page with a heart full of thanks. Until then, may your days be filled with moments that make your gratitude list grow and your heart overflow with appreciation.

Chapter 6. Nurturing Relationships- The Art of Cultivating Connection

Hey there, relationship enthusiast! Get ready to dive into a chapter that's all about the beautiful dance of human connections. Whether it's with family, friends, or that special someone, relationships are the vibrant threads that weave the tapestry of our lives. In this chapter, we'll explore the art of nurturing relationships—how to water the garden of connection, tend to the bonds that matter, and watch them blossom into something truly extraordinary.

The Importance of Connection

Relationships are the heartbeat of our existence. They bring joy, support, and a sense of belonging to our lives. Science even tells us that strong social connections contribute to increased happiness, better mental health, and even a longer life. So, let's roll up our sleeves and delve into the art of cultivating meaningful connections.

Building Blocks of Nurturing Relationships

Just like a well-tended garden requires care and attention, so do our relationships. Let's explore the foundational building blocks that contribute to the growth and flourishing of connections.

1. *Communication is Key:* The backbone of any healthy relationship is effective communication. It's not just about words; it's about active listening, understanding, and expressing yourself authentically. Create spaces for open, honest conversations where everyone's voice is heard and valued.

2. *Empathy and Understanding:* Step into each other's shoes and see the world from their perspective. Empathy fosters deep understanding and emotional connection. It's the glue that binds relationships during both joyous and challenging times.

3. *Quality Time:* In our fast-paced lives, time is a precious commodity. Dedicate quality time to your relationships—whether it's a heart-to-heart

conversation, a shared meal, or a weekend adventure. Presence speaks louder than words.

4. *Trust as the Foundation:* Trust is the bedrock of strong relationships. It's built over time through consistent actions, reliability, and honesty. Trust creates a safe space for vulnerability and authentic connection.

Nurturing Family Bonds

Family is often our first and most enduring connection. Let's explore ways to nurture and strengthen those familial ties.

1. *Traditions and Rituals:* Establishing family traditions and rituals creates a sense of continuity and belonging. Whether it's a weekly game night, holiday traditions, or shared meals, these rituals build a foundation of shared experiences.

2. *Quality Family Time:* In the hustle of daily life, carving out intentional family time is crucial. It could be a weekend outing, a movie night, or even a simple dinner together. What matters is

the presence and connection during those moments.

3. *Communication in the Family:* Families thrive on healthy communication. Create an atmosphere where everyone feels comfortable expressing themselves. Regular family meetings can be a forum for open discussions, ensuring that everyone's voice is heard.

Nurturing Friendships

Friends are the chosen family, the kindred spirits who walk beside us on life's journey. Here's how to tend to these precious bonds.

1. *Regular Check-Ins:* Life gets busy, but taking a few minutes to check in with friends can make a world of difference. Send a text, make a call, or schedule a coffee catch-up. Regular communication maintains the thread of connection.

2. *Celebrate Milestones:* Whether it's birthdays, job promotions, or personal achievements, celebrate your friends' milestones. Acknowledge their

victories, and be there to offer support during challenges. Shared joy is doubled, and shared burdens are lightened.

3. *Quality One-on-One Time:* While group gatherings are fantastic, don't underestimate the power of one-on-one time. It allows for deeper conversations and strengthens the individual bonds within the group.

Nurturing Romantic Relationships

Ah, romance—the realm of butterflies, shared dreams, and stolen glances. Here's how to keep the flame burning bright.

1. *Express Love Daily:* Love is an ongoing practice, not a one-time event. Express your love daily through words, gestures, and acts of kindness. A simple "I love you" or a thoughtful gesture can go a long way.

2. *Date Nights:* In the midst of life's demands, don't forget to prioritize date nights. Whether it's a candlelit dinner, a movie night, or a spontaneous adventure, date nights keep the romance alive.

3. _Effective Conflict Resolution:_ Disagreements are inevitable, but how we navigate them defines the health of a relationship. Practice effective conflict resolution by staying calm, actively listening, and finding solutions together.

Balancing Independence and Togetherness

Nurturing relationships involves finding the delicate balance between independence and togetherness. It's about honoring each other's individuality while fostering a sense of unity.

1. _Pursue Individual Hobbies:_ Encourage each other to pursue individual hobbies and interests. This not only allows for personal growth but also brings fresh energy into the relationship.

2. _Shared Goals and Dreams:_ Identify shared goals and dreams that you can work towards as a team. Whether it's planning a trip, buying a home, or pursuing a joint project, shared aspirations create a sense of purpose and unity.

3. *Respect Boundaries:* Everyone needs personal space. Respect each other's boundaries, and communicate openly about your needs for alone time or moments of solitude.

Nurturing Professional Relationships

While personal relationships are often in the spotlight, professional connections play a significant role in our lives. Here's how to cultivate a positive work environment.

1. *Effective Communication:* Clear and open communication is crucial in the workplace. It fosters collaboration, minimizes misunderstandings, and contributes to a positive team culture.

2. *Recognition and Appreciation:* Acknowledge the contributions of your colleagues. A simple "thank you" or recognizing someone's effort in a meeting goes a long way in building a positive work environment.

3. *Team-Building Activities:* Organize team-building activities that go beyond the confines of the

office. Whether it's a team lunch, a retreat, or a collaborative project, these activities build camaraderie and strengthen professional bonds.

Overcoming Relationship Challenges

No relationship is without its challenges. Let's address common hurdles and explore strategies for overcoming them.

Communication Breakdowns: If communication becomes strained, take a step back and reassess. Practice active listening, express your thoughts calmly, and be open to feedback. Seeking the assistance of a mediator or counselor can also provide valuable insights.

Mismatched Expectations: Misaligned expectations can lead to disappointment. Foster open conversations about each other's expectations, and work together to find common ground. It's about understanding and aligning your goals and desires.

Balancing Priorities: In our hectic lives, balancing personal, professional, and social priorities can be challenging. Regularly reassess and communicate about priorities, ensuring that each aspect of life receives the attention it deserves.

The Gift of Forgiveness

Forgiveness is a potent elixir for the wounds that inevitably arise in relationships. It doesn't mean condoning hurtful actions but freeing yourself from the burden of resentment.

1. *Release Resentment:* Holding onto resentment is like carrying a heavy backpack. Forgiveness is the act of unburdening yourself from the weight of past grievances. It's a gift you give to yourself.

2. *Communication is Key:* If forgiveness feels challenging, communicate openly with the other person. Share your feelings, express your needs, and work together towards healing.

3. *Self-Forgiveness:* Don't forget to extend the gift of forgiveness to yourself. We're all human, prone

to mistakes. Learn from them, forgive yourself, and move forward with compassion.

Your Relationship Garden

As we conclude this chapter, envision your relationships as a garden—a vibrant, ever-evolving landscape that requires attention, care, and the occasional pruning. The art of nurturing relationships is an ongoing practice, one that involves tending to the unique needs of each connection in your life.

So, dear reader, may your relationships be a source of joy, support, and shared laughter. As you cultivate the gardens of connection in your life, may they flourish with the beauty of understanding, the resilience of trust, and the fragrance of love. Until the next chapter, go forth and tend to the garden of your relationships, sowing seeds of connection and reaping the abundant harvest of shared moments. Happy nurturing!

Chapter 7. Finding Joy in Work and Passion- Crafting a Fulfilling Career and Pursuing What Sets Your Soul on Fire

Hey there, fellow adventurer on the road to joy and fulfillment! Welcome to a chapter that's all about weaving joy into the fabric of your work and infusing passion into every endeavor. Whether you're navigating the realms of your career or exploring the landscapes of your deepest passions, this chapter is your guide to creating a life where every day feels like a step towards your heart's desires.

The Quest for Joy in Work

For many, work constitutes a significant portion of our lives. So, why not infuse it with joy and purpose? Let's embark on a journey to discover the keys to finding joy in your professional endeavors.

The Power of Purpose

At the heart of finding joy in work is the discovery of purpose. Purpose is the North Star that guides your professional journey, providing meaning and fulfillment. Here's how to uncover and align with your purpose:

1. *Reflect on Values:* What are the values that matter most to you? Reflect on principles that resonate with your core beliefs. Your purpose often aligns with the things that matter deeply to you.

2. *Identify Strengths:* What are your strengths and unique skills? Recognizing your strengths allows you to leverage them in your work, creating a sense of mastery and accomplishment.

3. *Impact and Contribution:* Consider the impact you want to make in the world. What contribution do you aspire to make? Finding work that aligns with your desire to make a positive difference can be deeply fulfilling.

Crafting a Joyful Work Environment

The environment in which you work plays a significant role in your overall sense of joy and satisfaction. Let's explore how to cultivate a positive and joyful workplace:

1. *Cultivate Positive Relationships:* Forge connections with colleagues who uplift and inspire you. Positive relationships contribute to a supportive and collaborative work environment.

2. *Celebrate Achievements:* Acknowledge and celebrate your achievements, no matter how small. Positive reinforcement fosters a sense of accomplishment and motivates you to continue striving for excellence.

3. *Balance and Well-Being:* Strive for a healthy work-life balance. Prioritize self-care, set boundaries, and take breaks to recharge. A balanced life enhances your overall well-being and contributes to lasting joy in your work.

Passion Projects and Side Hustles

While joy in work often begins with your primary career, passion projects and side hustles provide an additional canvas for creative expression and fulfillment.

1. *Identify Your Passion:* What activities set your soul on fire? Identify your passions, whether they are related to your current work or entirely separate pursuits.

2. *Start Small:* You don't need to dive headfirst into a new venture. Start small by exploring your passion through side projects or hobbies. This allows you to test the waters without overwhelming yourself.

3. *Embrace Learning:* Pursuing a passion often involves acquiring new skills and knowledge. Embrace the learning process, and view challenges as opportunities for growth.

The Dance of Joy and Productivity

Contrary to the notion that joy and productivity are at odds, they can be dance partners in the realm of work. Let's explore how to harmonize joy and productivity in your professional life:

1. *Set Meaningful Goals:* Align your professional goals with your sense of purpose. Meaningful goals inspire motivation and create a sense of accomplishment.

2. *Embrace Mindfulness:* Incorporate mindfulness practices into your work routine. Whether it's taking mindful breaks, practicing deep breathing, or incorporating moments of reflection, mindfulness enhances focus and productivity.

3. *Foster a Positive Mindset:* Cultivate a positive mindset towards your work. Focus on what you can control, acknowledge your achievements, and approach challenges with a solution-oriented mindset.

The Pursuit of Passion

Passion is the fuel that propels us towards our dreams. Whether it's a hobby, a side project, or a full-fledged career change, pursuing your passion is a courageous and fulfilling journey.

Identifying Your Passion

Discovering your passion is often a journey of self-exploration. Here are steps to help you identify and connect with your passion:

1. _Explore Your Interests:_ What activities make you lose track of time? Explore a variety of interests to discover what resonates with you on a deep level.

2. _Reflect on Childhood Dreams:_ Often, our childhood dreams hold clues to our true passions. Reflect on what you loved to do as a child, and consider how those interests can be integrated into your adult life.

3. _Connect with Your Values:_ Your passions are often intertwined with your core values. Identify the values that matter most to you, and explore how your passions align with these principles.

Turning Passion into Action

Identifying your passion is just the beginning. Here's how to turn that passion into a tangible, fulfilling reality:

1. *Set Clear Goals:* Define clear and achievable goals related to your passion. Whether it's starting a blog, learning a new skill, or launching a side business, articulate your vision.

2. *Create a Plan:* Develop a plan to systematically work towards your goals. Break down your larger vision into actionable steps, and create a timeline to track your progress.

3. *Embrace the Learning Journey:* Pursuing your passion often involves acquiring new knowledge and skills. Embrace the learning journey with curiosity and a growth mindset.

Balancing Passion and Practicality

While pursuing your passion is invigorating, it's essential to balance your dreams with practical considerations. Here's how to strike a balance between passion and practicality:

1. *Create a Financial Plan:* Assess the financial implications of pursuing your passion. Develop a financial plan that includes a budget, savings, and contingency funds to support your journey.

2. _Start Small:_ You don't need to make drastic changes overnight. Start small by integrating your passion into your current routine or exploring it as a side project. This allows you to test the waters while maintaining stability.

3. _Seek Professional Advice:_ If your passion involves a significant career change, seek advice from professionals in the field. Networking and mentorship can provide valuable insights and guidance.

Overcoming Challenges on the Journey

The pursuit of joy in work and passion is not without its challenges. Let's address common obstacles and explore strategies to overcome them:

Fear of Failure: Fear of failure can be paralyzing. Embrace the mindset that failure is a natural part of the learning process. View setbacks as opportunities for growth, and remember that each failure brings you one step closer to success.

External Pressures: External pressures, whether from societal expectations or well-meaning advice, can create internal conflict. Tune into your own values and aspirations, and make decisions that align with your authentic self.

Impatience for Results: The journey towards joy and fulfillment takes time. Impatience for immediate results can lead to frustration. Cultivate patience, celebrate small victories, and trust the process of gradual growth.

Savoring the Journey

As we wrap up this chapter, remember that the journey towards joy in work and passion is as significant as the destination. Savor each step, celebrate the progress you make, and embrace the joy that unfolds along the way.

So, dear reader, may your work be a source of inspiration and fulfillment, and may your passions be the guiding stars of your journey. As you navigate the realms of career and personal pursuits, may each day bring you closer to a life that reflects your truest desires. Until the next chapter, go forth with joy in your heart and passion in your stride. Happy exploring!

Chapter 8. Physical Well-Being for a Happy Mind-Nourishing Your Body, Energizing Your Spirit

Hey there, wellness warrior! Get ready to embark on a chapter that's all about the beautiful dance between a happy mind and a healthy body. We're diving into the realm of physical well-being, exploring how taking care of your body can be a cornerstone for a joyful and vibrant life.

The Mind-Body Connection

Imagine your body and mind as dance partners, moving in harmony with the rhythm of life. Physical well-being isn't just about appearances; it's about nurturing a strong connection between your body and your mind. Let's unravel the secrets of this intricate dance.

Nourishing Your Body

Fueling your body with the right nutrients is like giving it a daily dose of love. Here's how to create a nourishing relationship with the vessel that carries you through life:

1. *Balanced Nutrition:* Embrace a balanced and varied diet that includes a rainbow of fruits, vegetables, whole grains, lean proteins, and healthy fats. Each nutrient plays a unique role in supporting your overall health.

2. *Hydration is Key:* Water is not just a beverage; it's a lifeline for your body. Stay hydrated to support bodily functions, maintain energy levels, and keep your skin radiant.

3. *Mindful Eating:* Slow down and savor each bite. Mindful eating involves paying attention to the colors, textures, and flavors of your food. It not only enhances the dining experience but also fosters a healthier relationship with food.

The Joy of Movement

Exercise isn't just a task on your to-do list; it's a celebration of what your body can do. Let's explore how movement can become a source of joy and vitality:

1. _Find Activities You Love:_ Exercise doesn't have to mean hitting the gym if that's not your jam. Find activities that bring you joy—whether it's dancing, hiking, yoga, or playing a sport. When you love what you do, it doesn't feel like a chore.

2. _Make it Social:_ Exercise becomes even more enjoyable when shared with others. Join a fitness class, go for a walk with a friend, or play a team sport. The camaraderie adds an extra layer of fun to your physical activities.

3. _Build Consistency:_ Rather than intense sporadic workouts, focus on consistent movement. Whether it's a daily walk, a weekly dance session, or a weekend hike, consistency is key to reaping the long-term benefits of exercise.

Prioritizing Sleep

Ah, the sweet embrace of sleep—your body's way of recharging and rejuvenating. Quality sleep is a non-negotiable for a happy mind and a healthy body:

1. _Create a Relaxing Bedtime Routine:_ Wind down before sleep with calming activities such as

reading, gentle stretching, or listening to soothing music. Create a bedtime routine that signals to your body that it's time to rest.

2. _Limit Screen Time:_ The blue light emitted by screens can interfere with your sleep-wake cycle. Aim to reduce screen time at least an hour before bedtime to promote better sleep.

3. _Prioritize Consistent Sleep Schedule:_ Go to bed and wake up at the same time every day, even on weekends. Consistency helps regulate your body's internal clock, improving the quality of your sleep.

Stress Management and Relaxation

Stress is an inevitable part of life, but how you manage it makes all the difference. Let's explore strategies to keep stress in check and invite relaxation into your daily routine:

1. _Mindfulness and Meditation:_ These practices are like a mini-vacation for your mind. Incorporate mindfulness or meditation into your day to

promote relaxation, reduce stress, and enhance mental clarity.

2. *Breathing Exercises:* The breath is a powerful tool for stress management. Practice deep breathing exercises to activate the body's relaxation response. It's a simple yet effective way to calm your nervous system.

3. *Create Relaxation Rituals:* Whether it's a warm bath, listening to calming music, or spending time in nature, create rituals that help you unwind and release tension.

Building Healthy Habits

Healthy habits are the building blocks of physical well-being. Let's explore how to cultivate habits that contribute to a happy mind and body:

1. *Start Small:* Rome wasn't built in a day, and neither are habits. Start with small, manageable changes, and gradually build upon them. This approach makes it more likely for habits to stick.

2. *Set Realistic Goals:* Be kind to yourself by setting realistic and achievable goals. Break larger goals

into smaller milestones, and celebrate your progress along the way.

3. *Stay Consistent:* Consistency is the secret sauce of habit formation. Whether it's adopting a new exercise routine, improving your diet, or establishing a sleep schedule, stay consistent for lasting results.

Listening to Your Body

Your body is a wise guide that communicates its needs. Tune in and listen to what it's telling you:

1. *Intuitive Eating:* Pay attention to your body's hunger and fullness cues. Eat when you're hungry, and stop when you're satisfied. Intuitive eating fosters a healthy relationship with food.

2. *Rest and Recovery:* Just as movement is essential, so is rest. Listen to your body's signals for rest and recovery. Adequate rest is crucial for preventing burnout and supporting overall well-being.

3. *Seek Professional Guidance:* If you're unsure about the best approach to physical well-being, consider seeking guidance from healthcare professionals, nutritionists, or fitness experts. They can provide personalized advice based on your unique needs.

The Holistic Approach

Physical well-being is not just about individual components; it's about embracing a holistic approach that considers the interconnectedness of mind, body, and spirit:

1. *Holistic Nutrition:* View nutrition as more than just counting calories. Consider the quality of your food, mindful eating practices, and the overall nourishment of your body.

2. *Mind-Body Practices:* Integrate mind-body practices such as yoga, tai chi, or qigong into your routine. These practices harmonize physical movement with mental focus, promoting holistic well-being.

3. *Cultivate Gratitude:* Gratitude isn't just for the mind; it's for the body too. Appreciate the capabilities of your body, its resilience, and the intricate processes that keep you alive and thriving.

Overcoming Physical Well-Being Challenges

Let's address common challenges that may hinder your journey to physical well-being and explore strategies to overcome them:

Time Constraints: In a busy world, finding time for physical well-being may feel challenging. Prioritize self-care by scheduling dedicated time for exercise, meal preparation, and relaxation.

Motivation Fluctuations: Motivation ebbs and flows. When you feel a dip in motivation, focus on the intrinsic rewards of physical well-being—how it makes you feel, the energy it provides, and the joy it brings.

Comparisons and Expectations: Avoid comparing your journey to others or setting unrealistic expectations. Your path to physical well-being is unique. Celebrate your progress and honor your individuality.

Your Joyful Body, Your Happy Mind

As we wrap up this chapter, remember that physical well-being is a journey, not a destination. It's a daily practice of self-love and self-care, a dance between the tangible and the intangible elements of your being.

So, dear reader, may your body be a source of joy, strength, and vitality. As you nourish it with wholesome foods, move it with love, and prioritize its well-being, may your mind dance in harmony, radiating happiness and contentment. Until the next chapter, continue to nurture the beautiful connection between your joyful body and your happy mind. Cheers to a life of well-being and vibrant health!

CHAPTER 9. EMBRACING IMPERFECTION- THE ART OF CELEBRATING YOUR BEAUTIFUL FLAWS

Hey there, fellow perfection-seeking soul! Welcome to a chapter that's all about tossing the pursuit of flawlessness out the window and embracing the delightful messiness of being human. Buckle up for a journey into the liberating world of imperfection, where quirks, mishaps, and unique flaws are not just accepted but celebrated.

The Myth of Perfection

Perfection—the elusive standard that often leaves us feeling like we're chasing a mirage. In this chapter, we're diving headfirst into the myth of perfection and exploring the beauty that emerges when we let go of the impossible quest for flawlessness.

The Weight of Perfectionism

Perfectionism, though often hailed as a virtue, can be a heavy burden to carry. Let's unpack the weighty consequences of striving for perfection:

1. *Fear of Failure:* The perfectionist's nightmare. The fear of making mistakes or falling short of impossibly high standards can paralyze us from taking risks and embracing new challenges.

2. *Self-Criticism:* Perfectionism often goes hand in hand with a harsh inner critic. Every perceived flaw or mistake becomes a reason for self-condemnation, eroding self-esteem and fostering a negative self-image.

3. *Procrastination:* Striving for perfection can lead to procrastination. The pressure to produce flawless work can create a paralysis that prevents us from starting or completing tasks.

The Joy of Imperfection

Now, let's turn the tables and explore the joyous realm of imperfection. What if, instead of perfection, we sought authenticity, growth, and the simple pleasure of being beautifully imperfect?

The Beauty in Flaws

Flaws aren't just cracks in the facade; they're the unique brushstrokes that make each person a masterpiece. Let's celebrate the beauty in our imperfections:

1. *Authenticity:* Imperfections are a testament to authenticity. They reveal the real, unfiltered you—the person behind the carefully curated image.

2. *Character and Charm:* What would life be without quirks and eccentricities? Imperfections add character and charm, making each individual a fascinating and multi-dimensional being.

3. *Humor and Lightness:* There's something inherently humorous and light-hearted about embracing imperfections. It's the ability to laugh at ourselves, finding joy in the delightful messiness of life.

The Art of Self-Compassion

In the quest for imperfection, self-compassion is your trusty guide. Here's how to cultivate a kinder, gentler relationship with yourself:

1. *Speak to Yourself Like a Friend:* Imagine if your inner dialogue mirrored the way you speak to your closest friend. Be a friend to yourself, offering words of encouragement, understanding, and support.

2. *Acknowledge Growth, Not Perfection:* Shift your focus from perfection to growth. Instead of aiming for flawlessness, celebrate the progress you make and the lessons learned along the way.

3. *Practice Mindfulness:* Mindfulness is a powerful tool for cultivating self-compassion. Be present with your thoughts and feelings, acknowledging them without judgment. This mindful awareness opens the door to self-acceptance.

Embracing Mistakes as Stepping Stones

Mistakes aren't roadblocks; they're stepping stones on the path of growth and discovery. Let's explore how to shift our perspective on mistakes:

1. *Learn and Grow:* Mistakes are rich with lessons. Instead of viewing them as failures, see them as opportunities to learn, adapt, and grow. Each misstep is a chance to refine your approach and move forward wiser.

2. *Release the Need for Perfection:* Perfection is an unattainable ideal. Release the need to be perfect, and instead, embrace the imperfect, messy, and wonderfully unpredictable journey of life.

3. *Courage in Vulnerability:* Embracing imperfection requires courage—the courage to be vulnerable, to show up authentically, and to acknowledge that, yes, you're beautifully flawed. This vulnerability fosters genuine connections with others who appreciate you for who you truly are.

Navigating External Pressures

In a world that often celebrates polished images and flawless personas, navigating external pressures to conform to societal expectations can be challenging.

Let's explore how to stay true to yourself amidst external influences:

1. *Define Your Own Standards:* Instead of succumbing to external standards, define your own. What does success, beauty, or achievement mean to you? Create standards that align with your values and aspirations.

2. *Surround Yourself with Authenticity:* Seek connections with individuals and communities that embrace authenticity. Surrounding yourself with people who appreciate imperfection fosters a supportive and genuine environment.

3. *Mindful Media Consumption:* Be mindful of the media you consume. Curate your digital and social media spaces to include content that celebrates realness and diversity. Unfollow accounts that perpetuate unrealistic standards.

Celebrating Uniqueness

Imperfections aren't cookie-cutter; they're uniquely yours. Let's celebrate the glorious tapestry of individuality:

1. *Diversity of Experiences:* Imperfections reflect the diversity of human experiences. What might be considered a flaw in one context could be a source of strength or beauty in another. Embrace the richness of these diverse narratives.

2. *Cultivate Self-Love:* Loving yourself, imperfections and all, is a transformative act. Treat yourself with the same kindness and affection you would offer to a cherished friend.

3. *Empathy for Others:* Just as you embrace your imperfections, extend that same empathy to others. Recognize and celebrate the uniqueness in those around you, fostering a culture of acceptance and appreciation.

The Liberation of Imperfection

Embracing imperfection isn't a one-time event; it's a lifelong journey. It's about continually letting go of the weight of perfection and embracing the liberation that comes with being beautifully, authentically imperfect.

Overcoming the Fear of Judgment

The fear of judgment often accompanies the embrace of imperfection. Let's address this fear and explore strategies for overcoming it:

1. *Shift Your Focus:* Instead of fixating on potential judgment, shift your focus to self-approval. When you genuinely accept yourself, external judgments carry less weight.

2. *Remember Your Worth:* Your worth isn't determined by the opinions of others. Remind yourself of your inherent value, regardless of external evaluations.

3. *Surround Yourself with Positivity:* Cultivate relationships with individuals who uplift and support you. Positive, affirming connections contribute to a sense of security and confidence.

The Imperfectly Perfect You

As we conclude this chapter, envision yourself as a unique masterpiece—imperfect brushstrokes, quirks, and all. Embrace the beautifully messy, wonderfully imperfect canvas that is you.

So, dear reader, may you revel in the joy of imperfection. May you dance with the delightful unpredictability of life, celebrating each flaw as a stroke of authenticity. As you continue on this journey, may your heart be light, your spirit be free, and your embrace of imperfection be a source of boundless joy. Until the next chapter, go forth with the confidence of someone who knows that imperfection is not the absence of perfection but a glorious masterpiece in its own right. Cheers to the imperfectly perfect you!

Chapter 10. Sustaining Happiness for a Lifetime- A Joyful Journey Into Forever Smiles

Welcome to the final chapter of our delightful journey toward a lifetime of joy. In this chapter, we're exploring the art of sustaining happiness, not as a fleeting emotion but as a companion for the long haul. Get ready for a friendly guide on how to weave happiness into the very fabric of your life, creating a tapestry of enduring smiles.

The Essence of Sustaining Happiness

Sustaining happiness is not about a constant state of euphoria; it's about cultivating a resilient and positive mindset that weathers the storms of life. Let's delve into the essence of sustaining happiness:

1. *Resilience in Adversity:* Life is a rollercoaster, and sustaining happiness requires resilience. It's the ability to bounce back from challenges, learn from setbacks, and maintain a positive outlook even in difficult times.

2. *Mindful Presence:* Happiness isn't just a destination; it's a way of traveling. Mindful presence involves fully experiencing and savoring each moment, whether it's a joyful celebration or a quiet, ordinary day.

3. *Gratitude as a Daily Practice:* Gratitude is the secret sauce of sustaining happiness. Regularly acknowledging and appreciating the positive aspects of your life cultivates a mindset of abundance and contentment.

Nurturing Positive Habits

Happiness is often a result of daily habits that nourish your mind, body, and spirit. Let's explore positive habits that contribute to the sustained joy in your life:

1. *Morning Rituals:* Start your day with intention. Whether it's a moment of gratitude, a morning walk, or a calming cup of tea, morning rituals set a positive tone for the rest of the day.

2. *Mindful Moments:* Throughout the day, incorporate mindful moments. It could be a deep

breath, a moment of reflection, or a pause to appreciate the beauty around you. Mindful moments anchor you in the present and enhance overall well-being.

3. *Acts of Kindness:* Engage in acts of kindness, both for yourself and others. Whether it's a small gesture of self-care, a compliment, or a helping hand, acts of kindness create a ripple effect of positivity.

Building Meaningful Connections

The tapestry of happiness is woven with the threads of meaningful connections. Let's explore how relationships contribute to sustained joy:

1. *Quality Time:* Invest in quality time with loved ones. Shared experiences and genuine connections with family and friends contribute to a sense of belonging and joy.

2. *Cultivating Empathy:* Empathy strengthens relationships and fosters a deeper understanding of others. Cultivate empathy by actively listening,

seeking to understand different perspectives, and offering support when needed.

3. *Expressing Love:* Love is a powerful source of happiness. Express your love regularly, whether through words, gestures, or acts of kindness. Love not only strengthens your connections but also enhances your own sense of well-being.

Pursuing Passion and Purpose

Passion and purpose add layers of fulfillment to the journey of happiness. Let's explore how to infuse your life with activities and pursuits that light up your soul:

1. *Identifying Passion:* Reflect on your passions and interests. What activities bring you joy and a sense of purpose? Identifying your passions is the first step toward integrating them into your life.

2. *Setting Meaningful Goals:* Align your goals with your values and passions. Meaningful goals provide a sense of purpose, motivation, and a

roadmap for your journey toward sustained happiness.

3. *Celebrating Achievements:* Acknowledge and celebrate your achievements, both big and small. Celebrations create a positive feedback loop, reinforcing your sense of accomplishment and joy.

Mind-Body Harmony

The connection between mind and body is a crucial aspect of sustaining happiness. Let's explore practices that promote holistic well-being:

1. *Regular Exercise:* Physical activity not only benefits your body but also has profound effects on your mental well-being. Find forms of exercise you enjoy and make them a regular part of your routine.

2. *Mindfulness and Meditation:* Mindfulness practices and meditation cultivate a calm and centered mind. Regular mindfulness exercises reduce stress, enhance focus, and contribute to an overall sense of peace.

3. *Adequate Rest:* Quality sleep is essential for sustained happiness. Prioritize a consistent sleep schedule, create a relaxing bedtime routine, and ensure your body gets the rest it deserves.

Finding Joy in Simple Pleasures

Happiness often resides in the simplicity of everyday moments. Let's explore the art of finding joy in the small and ordinary:

1. *Gratitude Journaling:* Keep a gratitude journal to document the simple pleasures and positive moments in your life. Regularly reflecting on these entries enhances your appreciation for the beauty around you.

2. *Mindful Awareness:* Practice mindful awareness in your daily activities. Whether it's savoring the flavor of your morning coffee or appreciating the warmth of sunlight, mindful presence amplifies the joy in simple moments.

3. *Nature Connection:* Spend time in nature. Whether it's a walk in the park, a hike in the mountains, or a moment by the ocean, nature has

a profound effect on your well-being and happiness.

Overcoming Challenges on the Journey

Sustaining happiness doesn't mean avoiding challenges; it means navigating them with resilience and grace. Let's address common challenges and explore strategies to overcome them:

Unexpected Setbacks: Life is unpredictable, and setbacks are inevitable. When faced with unexpected challenges, focus on what you can control, seek support, and maintain a positive mindset.

Comparison and Envy: The comparison game can hinder sustained happiness. Shift your focus from comparing yourself to others to appreciating your unique journey. Celebrate the successes of others without diminishing your own achievements.

Burnout and Overwhelm: In the pursuit of sustained happiness, it's crucial to avoid burnout. Prioritize self-care, set boundaries, and recognize when it's time to recharge and rejuvenate.

The Joyful Mindset

Sustaining happiness is not a destination; it's a way of approaching life with a joyful mindset. Let's explore the key components of this mindset:

1. _Optimism:_ Cultivate an optimistic outlook on life. Focus on the positive aspects of situations, practice gratitude, and approach challenges with a belief in your ability to overcome them.

2. _Adaptability:_ Life is ever-changing, and adaptability is a key to sustained happiness. Embrace change as a natural part of the journey, and view challenges as opportunities for growth.

3. _Mindful Resilience:_ Resilience is the ability to bounce back from adversity. Combine resilience with mindfulness, staying present with your thoughts and emotions, to navigate challenges with greater ease.

Creating Your Happiness Blueprint

As we wrap up this chapter and our journey together, it's time for you to craft your happiness blueprint. Consider the following steps:

1. *Reflect on Your Values:* What values are most important to you? Your happiness blueprint should align with your core values and aspirations.

2. *Identify Key Happiness Factors:* What activities, relationships, and experiences contribute most to your happiness? Identify the key factors that bring you joy and fulfillment.

3. *Set Intentional Goals:* Based on your reflections, set intentional goals for sustaining happiness. These goals can encompass various aspects of your life, from relationships to personal growth to well-being practices.

4. *Regularly Evaluate and Adjust:* Life is dynamic, and so is your happiness blueprint. Regularly evaluate your goals, celebrate achievements, and make adjustments as needed. Flexibility is key to sustained happiness.

Your Everlasting Journey of Joy

Congratulations on completing this journey toward sustained happiness! Remember, happiness is not a destination reached but a companion for the journey. Embrace the ebb and flow of life, celebrate the highs and navigate the lows with resilience and a joyful heart.

So, dear reader, may your days be filled with laughter, your heart be brimming with gratitude, and your spirit be buoyed by the enduring joy you've cultivated. As you continue your everlasting journey of happiness, may each step be a dance of joy, and may the tapestry of your life be woven with the vibrant colors of contentment and fulfillment. Until we meet again, go forth with a heart full of joy and a spirit that radiates the beauty of a life well-lived. Cheers to your boundless happiness!

"Embrace the simplicity of small changes, for in their subtle dance, lies the symphony of a profoundly happier you—a melody composed by the daily harmonies of joy, gratitude, and purpose."

Milton Keynes UK
Ingram Content Group UK Ltd.
UKHW022035301123
433552UK00015B/511